A LEG AT EACH CORNER

by Norman Thelwell

A LEG AT EACH CORNER

thelwell's
COMPLETE GUIDE TO EQUITATION

Mandarin

FOR
PENELOPE

A LEG AT EACH CORNER

First published in 1962 by Methuen & Co Ltd
Reprinted eight times

First paperback edition published 1969 by Eyre Methuen Ltd
Reprinted 1969 (twice), 1970 (twice), 1971 (twice), 1972 (twice),
1973, 1975, 1977, 1978, 1982, 1985, 1986, 1987
This paperback edition published in 1991
Reprinted 1991
by Mandarin Paperbacks,
Michelin House, 81 Fulham Road, London SW3 6RB

Methuen and Mandarin are imprints of the Octopus Publishing Group,
a division of Reed International Books Limited

Copyright © 1962 by Norman Thelwell

ISBN 0 7493 0947 4

A CIP catalogue record for this book
is available from the British Library

Printed and bound in Great Britain
by Cox & Wyman Ltd, Reading, Berkshire

This drawing reproduced by permission of the Proprietors of *Punch*

CONTENTS

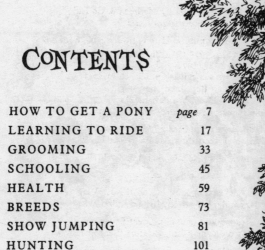

HOW TO GET A PONY

Acquiring a pony is not quite as easy as it sounds . . .

It is against the law to take them from the New Forest

– and risky to buy them from public auctions.

So look out for one which a friend has grown out of –

or buy one from
someone you trust.

When choosing . . .

good feet are most important

– and good manners
essential

– the eyes will tell you more
than any other feature . . .

but expert advice is needed as defects are often covered up.

Some ponies do not move well –

some do not move at all.

You will learn a great deal from a glance
at his teeth and remember –

never buy a horse that whistles.

You won't find your perfect
pony straight away –
but sooner or later . . .

. . . he'll find you.

LEARNING TO RIDE

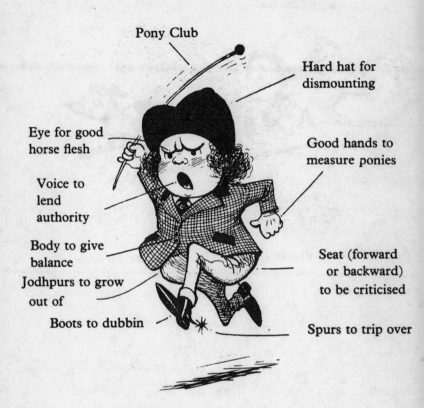

Pony Club

Hard hat for dismounting

Eye for good horse flesh

Good hands to measure ponies

Voice to lend authority

Body to give balance

Seat (forward or backward) to be criticised

Jodhpurs to grow out of

Boots to dubbin

Spurs to trip over

POINTS OF A RIDER

A child is ready to ride as soon as he shows himself keen . . .

but it is inadvisable to influence him against his will.

The method of mounting is not important . . .

. . . so long as it is safe.

The correct sitting position must be mastered

and exercises carried out in the saddle –

The natural aids to horsemanship are the hands,
the legs, the body and the voice –

The artificial aids . . .

are whips, spurs, martingales
and gags.

Grip will improve with experience

and balance
with practice –

Talk to your pony – he will know what you mean –

and spend as much time in his
company as you possibly can.

* * * * * * *

In spite of our
constant criticism
of children today

there is no doubt
that they have . . .

as much spirit of adventure – determination . . .

... and downright courage ...

. . . as their parents . . .

. . . ever had.

GROOMING

Make sure your pony is securely tied.

You will know when his coat needs attention –

– but don't clip him yourself unless
you are an expert.

Begin grooming by removing all surplus mud –

– and tone up his muscles by banging
with a sack of wet straw.

Use the body brush vigorously – he will enjoy it.

Polish his coat with a rubber.

Get his tail well into the bucket when shampooing –

But beware of washing the mane
just before a show.

Detergents should be avoided

and tail-pulling undertaken with care.

Finish off by applying bandages to the legs.

SCHOOLING

A happy pony thinks of you as his best friend

so never lose your temper over some little mistake

but have some tit-bit handy when he does well.

He must be taught to stand correctly –

– to be led without fuss

and to move off promptly, when ordered to do so.

He will quickly get used to having his bridle put on –

but you should put smaller weights on his back before attempting to mount him yourself.

Mastery is achieved by subtlety . . .

. . . not by abuse

but at least two people may be necessary to work
him on the lunge rein.

Ponies are natural jumpers

but don't expect miracles too early.

Endless patience is required –

and absolute authority must be maintained.

Once you have gained your pony's respect
half the battle is won.

HEALTH

Warble — Thrush

Humour
Sweet Itch
Colic

Strangles

Girth Gall
Saddle Sore

Splint

A FEW COMMON AILMENTS

If bored, ponies develop troublesome vices . . .

. . . so try to keep him entertained.

If simple ailments are detected –

don't panic

make him warm and comfortable

keep a few simple remedies handy

and learn how to administer them.

Colds can be relieved by inhaling eucalyptus –

and coughs by smearing the back
of the tongue with paste.

If he is constantly trying to scratch himself,
suspect skin trouble

and if he rolls about, it is probably colic.

Sympathetic nursing can work wonders –

but don't try to replace the vet.

You will know it has all been worth it
when he's up and about again.

BREEDS

The NEW FOREST pony lives almost exclusively on
a diet of lettuce, cucumber and fish-paste sandwiches.

Owing to the harshness of its environment the
DARTMOOR has become tough and hardy.

The **EXMOOR** is mealy-mouthed.

The WELSH MOUNTAIN – our most beautiful
native breed – is inclined to be a trifle
wide in the barrel.

The ancient CONNEMARA was hanging
about Galway Bay long before the
song-writers got there.

FELL AND DALE can carry prodigious weights with ease.

The HIGHLAND is used
by sportsmen to carry
their 'bag' down the
mountains.

The SHETLAND – which is the world's
smallest breed . . .

. . . is respected by all who know horse flesh.

There are other ponies too – known as
BLOOD PONIES.

They can be seen in action at horse shows
all over the country.

SHOW JUMPING

Competitors must enter the arena mounted.

They may adopt the forward seat . . .

. . . or the backward seat

but they must not start until the signal is given . . .

. . . or stop before completing the course.

No more than three refusals are permitted –

and no foot must touch the water.

Blinkers are not allowed –

and unauthorised assistance is prohibited.

Don't expect to win every time . . .

. . . your turn will come.

*   *   *   *   *

HOW TO TIME YOUR JUMPS

Take-off
too early
◀

Take-off
too late
◀

Take-off just right

There is no doubt at all in the
minds of horse lovers . . .

that the long hours of patient training . . .

. . . laborious work . . .

. . . careful grooming . . .

. . . are amply repaid . . .

. . . by the thrill of attending . . .

. . . a gymkhana.

HUNTING

Nose for
'owning'
the
scent

Head for
'Throwing up'

'Stern'
for
'feathering'

'Voice' to
'give tongue'

A HALF COUPLE OF HOUNDS

Scent

Brush

Mask

'CHARLES JAMES' OR 'THE VARMINT'

A smart turnout is of first importance.

See that your pony arrives at the meet quite fresh.

Don't wait until the secretary
asks before you pay your 'cap' –

and give the master a polite greeting when you see him.

The fox is frequently referred to by other names –

but a hound is a hound and must never be called anything else.

Always do exactly what the huntsman tells you . . .

and if you must talk in the field – make it a whisper.

Don't monopolise the best fences –

and even if you're able to keep up with the hounds . . .

you're not a real rider until you've been blooded.

POINTS TO REMEMBER

An untidy rider is an insult to a horse.

Do nothing which may cause him alarm –

but he should be introduced
to the hazards of modern
traffic.

An active pony will need shoeing regularly.

Keep something handy to pick out his hooves.

Make sure that his tack fits snugly – or it may chafe

and always check the girth before you move off.

and always check the girth before you make off

Don't jump fences too close to trees –

– or leave gates open after going through them.

Keep a sharp lookout for signs of lice –

and if he's a kicker you must tie a red ribbon on his tail.

When you win something – don't take all the credit yourself . . .

. . . remember who did most of the work.

Don't keep him out when he wants to go home

and always attend to his comfort before your own.

In short – treat your pony as you like
to be treated yourself.